M A D E
I N
R O A T H
Volume One

Various Authors
and Contributors

Edited by
Christina Thatcher

First Printing, 2015

ISBN 10: 1-904958-46-X

ISBN 13: 978-1-904958-46-8

published by

*Opening Chapter
Cardiff, Wales*

www.openingchapter.com

Cover photograph by Nigel Pugh

Cover Design by Andrew Jones

To Roath, with love.

Tell us a secret about Roath.

Roath tells its own secrets. Just listen.

Christina Thatcher

Contents

Introduction

Like so many Cardiff residents, the love I have for Roath grows stronger each time I visit. I have written more poetry about this place than anywhere else in Wales. Not only because I was the writer-in-residence at the Milkwood Gallery (which has now lovingly been transformed into Cardiff MADE), but because there is something unique and wonderful about this community.

Beneath the diverse shop fronts and rows of terraced houses lies a thriving network of artists, writers, film-makers, and other creatives brought together by the vibrancy contained in this neighbourhood. It is hard to say what specifically drew these people here – the many parks, the Victorian architecture, the exciting food – but, whatever it was, the love Roath residents have for their home is nothing short of inspiring.

It is for all these reasons and more that Made in Roath thrives in this unique part of Cardiff. This free festival aims to bring art and the community closer together by showcasing the work of emerging and established musicians, artists, writers, and performers. Each year, these creatives volunteer their time to share their work with the community through various events. Residents get involved too by opening up their homes to exhibit art, host performances, and deliver workshops. The support, kindness, and generosity of everyone involved is humbling.

Over the past few years Made in Roath has grown to touch the lives of many different people. It gives new artists a chance to exhibit their work, new writers a chance to read, and new performers a stage they can call their own. The inclusive and dynamic nature of Made in Roath means that groups who do not normally have a voice are given one. Small businesses are celebrated and anything homemade is encouraged. During the festival, more than any other time of year, the community hums with an inspiring kind of activity and excitement.

Made in Roath reflects the enthusiasm and collective spirit of this very special neighbourhood. Whatever your interest – be it art, literature, music, performance, or something wonderfully different – you will find something to love there. And, we hope here, in the very first book that aims to capture, in words and photographs, all that is wonderful about Made in Roath.

Christina Thatcher
Made in Roath Poetry and Literature Coordinator

About the festival

Made in Roath is an artist-led, free event which aims to take art out of the gallery and into the wider community, allowing a larger and broader audience to access the wealth of creative talent in our neighbourhood whilst maintaining a standard of excellence, reflecting the contemporary art scene in Cardiff and South Wales.

It showcases the work of emerging and established artists, makers, musicians, writers and performers, who use the whole of Roath as the venue, including domestic, commercial, public and overlooked or disused spaces.

Made in Roath offers residents and visitors an opportunity to engage in the arts through a dynamic programme of exhibitions, residencies, collaborations with community groups, workshops and performances.

For more information please visit the Made in Roath website http://madeinroath.com/. You can also like them on Facebook, follow them on Twitter or just come along to their next exciting endeavour in Cardiff.

Note from the publisher - October 2015

This is a sort of explanation, an excuse, an apology.

Dear contributors and readers,

This book was originally intended for publication before the "Made in Spring" part of "Made in Roath" in May this year. There are many reasons for its lateness, none of them are due to the tardiness of the organisers or the contributors.

Perhaps the stars weren't aligned correctly or the planet's magnetic poles were oscillating too rapidly; but more than likely in this specific version of the universe** there was no space for a publication such as this at that time.

Maybe there's still no appropriate space-time-space, but we'll squash it in anyway – let's just hope it doesn't screw up the time-space-continuum too much.

Anyway – there's obviously oodles of creative energy and talent in or associated with the area of human habitation known as Roath – this book is just a snapshot of a particular subset of it taken from a particular angle at a particular time.

** Note: It's entirely possible and probably probable that we make our own universes.

Yours in quantum truth
Derec Jones, Opening Chapter

IMPORTANT NOTICE ABOUT NECESSARY CHAOS
During the 12 months or so since we received the material from the contributors it has somehow got mixed up – so if things appear to be separated from their related things they probably are.

Made in Roath Book Contributors

clare e. potter

clare e. potter is a writer, performer and educator from Cefn Fforest. She spent ten years in the Deep South where she did an MA in Afro-Caribbean literature. She teaches creative writing at Cardiff University and won the John Tripp Award for Spoken Poetry. Her work as been published in Planet, New Welsh Review, Wales Arts Review, Mslexia, Cahoots Magazine, Cambrensis, The Seminary Ridge Review Journal and various anthologies. Her first poetry collection is spilling histories. Last year, she received a bursary from Literature Wales and has written a subsequent collection, A Certain Darkness. She has written for the Welsh National Opera in community theatre and singing projects, and has received various commissions to write poetry in collaboration with artists. She has read at the Hay Festival and at the Smithsonian Folk-Life Festival. She is currently ghost writing a memoir and will be writing a collection of poetry in Welsh.

Let it Rain

This Roath City, Wellfield, Albany.
Fill your bags here.
No need to leave.
Even the gulls have given up
thoughts of sea to glide
above sleeping Scots. Though
there are rumbles, I hear,
on Angus. Fill your bags here
and listen: the children
are setting poems alight.
And the sky is full of them.

clare e. potter

Fran Smith

With 30 years working as a Holistic Therapist, Frances Smith writes about emotional links between mind, body and spirit. Fran conveys ideas with an appreciation and love for all creation, in particular the miracle of life in the human body. Fran advocates for animal welfare, protection of nature and environment, anti-abuse, stress and social welfare. Fran likes to convey links between all creation with the healing power of positive love for a more connected empathic world with unity and peace. She is a published writer and poet and has two books available on Amazon — Healing Poems for Positive Love and Book of Life and reads regularly at spoken word events.

www.francessmithwilliams.co.uk

Photo: Fran Smith

Chrissy Derbyshire at RARA goes story telling.

Rachel Simons

Rachel Simons is a Swansea ex-pat living in Roath. She mostly writes poetry and finds it a really exciting, social art form. She works in a homeless hostel and as well as writing she also enjoys gardening drawing+ cooking.

I've lived in Roath since 2007. At first I truly hated it. I came to study at the University and was attacked in my second term. After this I suffered with depression and desperately wanted to go home. I lived very much in the 'student bubble' and didn't think very much of my surroundings. I graduated in 2010; into the inauspicious climate of a "record high" of youth unemployment and though I lived with my partner, I was pretty lonely.

When I moved into my lovely, sunny flat on City Road I started appreciating Roath. I'd spend hours on our balcony (actually the top of the shop below, which we accessed by climbing out of the window) watching the people go past. Each night on my way home from work the man in the kebab shop downstairs would wave at me from his shop. There's a poem I've read at a few open mic nights, *The House That Alf Built,* that expresses how I feel about this special time. I started to take pleasure in noticing little details in my environment like the tiles above City Road Tesco, the spooky house at the end of Glenroy Street and the old signage on the back wall of the house at the corner of Treharris Street.

I didn't really know many people in my local community until I joined Roath Writers. Meeting other like minded people was an absolute godsend. Soon, I was hearing about lovely local restaurants, gigs, poetry nights and art exhibitions. I joined in with all I could and soon I found myself able to walk down Albany Road and say hello to people I knew. At last, I felt a sense of real connection to and pride in my local community.

The Made in Roath festival is a really special event because it enhances that feeling of community. You can feel yourself smiling at people, whether or not you know them! It's a time of hidden surprises, where you can follow a big red dot into someone's house and find that your neighbour is a wicked ceramicist.

However, life in Roath isn't only boating on the lake and independent coffee shops. I work as a support worker in a local homeless hostel and we see a lot of the entrenched social problems in our area including drugs, gangs and poverty. Working in this sector gives me a lot of pride that I'm working to ameliorate problems in my community. I always encourage my clients to develop links in their community because I believe it can have a very positive effect on the individual, as it has for me.

- Rachel Simons

Death Junction
For St. John Lloyd

The ghost leaves the bank
and walks into the road
with the recklessness of the drunk
or the dead.

He passes the Victorian hotel,
Polish supermarket and dusty record shop.
He stands with arms outstretched
on the cross where the four roads meet.

"I never was a good speaker in my life" he says.
Born in Breconshire, he watched the hills
from his gallows and is glad that even now
their green heads have not been swallowed,
like Jonah, by the city.

"I never was a good speaker in my life" he says.
The two priests waited for the gallows to be built.
A wait so long they were released
to buy apples and play tennis. A wait so long
they saw freedom bursting
like land from the hard line of the sea.

"I never was a good speaker in my life" he says,
now death has loosened his tongue.
He rounds on the cars and shouts –
how he watched his cell-mate's young blood
drying and dulling in the high July sun and how
he gave Evans the gift of delivering his last
sermon without the shake that comes
from seeing another man's legs dangle.

"I never was a good speaker in my life,"
he says.

Rachel Simons

The Gaiety, City Road

The pavements are cooling, the days heat
hits my legs like dog's breath.
Kurdish barbers bring chairs on the pavements,
cars nudge like clumsy lovers:
the whole long street starts to smell
of grilled meat and shisha smoke.

There's a new beat throbbing
from the derelict theatre opposite our flat,
police cars under the awnings
of our landlord's sari shop.
Smiling boys straddle blue domes
that in 1912 looked modern. They shout
to the street for music suggestions,
unroll bed sheets scrawled with
A.C.A.B.   FUCK THE POLICE.

All evening we watch the stand-off
against the rhubarb sunset.
On the roof the boys dance,
long limbed shadows leap
tall and fierce as gods.

Rachel Simons

After the Squatters

Came the man who slept under the awning;
lived life on the stage of City Road.
Each morning he swept his pavement,
sipped coffee, angled his face to the sun
while more items shored up beside him.

Once we woke to a sofa on the street;
Our man and his friends grinning,
bare toes brushing the legs of passers-by.
The landlord built a fence to keep him out.
He climbed in; after that we saw him only
through folds of tarpaulin,
staring out like a bear.
Finally the landlord came with a machine
and a skip, the fence and the shelter
crumbled like an empty snail shell.
Out slopped a pool of coffee cups,
newspapers, a table, a rucksack and a toy pram.

Rachel Simons

This [singing] led to a wonderful form of abstract freedom, very akin to childhood play, as many in the group acknowledged afterwards, commenting that they 'didn't care what I sounded like', that the session was 'trance-like' and 'shut the clatter out.' Everyone commented on the communal nature of the activity, and even after only spending half an hour in their company, I felt very connected to my fellow singers.

– Rebecca Roy, Made in Roath Blogger

More about the blog team at:

http://madeinroathblog.blogspot.co.uk/

photo: Fran Smith

Marc Montinaro at RARA goes story telling.

What do you think it is about Made in Roath, which makes it so distinctive a festival as it is?

It's hyper-local, community based work with a real longevity. Helen and Gail have worked so hard to get it to the point where people really recognise it, and love taking part. It's a real muddle of art and community, community and art.

- Clare Charles, Made in Roath Exhibitions Coordinator

Simon L. Read

Simon L. Read is an author, artist, performance poet, comedian, and coffee addict from Cardiff. He studied 'English and Creative Writing' at Cardiff Metropolitan University and has other qualifications in other things from other educational institutions.

Twitter: @SimonLRead

Made in...

I travelled
to Arbroath
for the festival...

then
to Roath,
embarrassed.

Simon L. Read

The Oddly Titled 'Cider and Seduction' Event (as performed at)

I aim
to entice
those apples.

Simon L. Read

photo Fran Smith

Ade Jones and Steve Jonzy at Scratch Platform

Will
Ford

Will Ford is a writer, spoken word performer, event organiser and host. Exploring the silly and the serious with equal voraciousness, his aim is to keep you wondering what he will say next. Will it move, amuse or unsettle? Website and blog details at www.willdeanford.com

3 Acronyms M.A.D.E.I.N.R.O.A.T.H

Momentarily After Darkness, Every Inch Notorious
Reducing Our Aspirations To Heartbeats

Maybe All Dreads End In Necessary
Reassurance Of A Taming Hand

Mighty As Daylight, Evening Is No
Ruler Of Any True Heart

Will Ford

ZOMBIE PARENTHOOD BLUES

The following is the song that closes the story of the same title, read publicly for the first time during Made in Roath 2014, at Rhyme and Real Ale Go Storytelling 20/10/2014 a t The Mackintosh Sports Club. People laughed regularly and at the song. They were meant to.

Zombie Dad sings:
Don't got no worries about income tax
Just stalk the night a-swinging my axe
Burying it in people's heads and backs
What else would a Zombie do?

And if we inflict excruciating pain
We're sorry but we need to feed on your brains
So if you try to get away we'll just catch you again
And turn you into Zombies too

Zombie Mum sings:
It's hard to be a Zombie Mum
Raising your kids to be ignorant scum
When all they wanna do is just help everyone
And tolerate other views

Both sing:
Our son has yet to butcher anyone
Our daughter don't possess
Even a set o' thumb screws
Got the low down, dirty
Kids growing up good
Zombie Parenthood Blues...

Will Ford

Spaces Between Them

The following was spoken, whispered and breathed into a microphone during Made in Roath 2014, at Cider and Seduction Open Mic, 16/10/2014 at the Roath Park Pub. The rest of the open mic slot was filled by a piece called Cider and Seduction, The Booty Song and a cover of Slow by Depeche Mode, sung a capella.

The individual heartbeats and breaths
And the spaces between them
Grew smaller as pupils began to dilate
Souls crossing the spaces between them

Corpuscles of blood racing to where
The sweetest of spaces between them
Might be rapidly filled, then emptied, then filled
If they closed other spaces between them

Words of pure nonsense
Were not pointed out
As they danced
In the spaces between them
Words from their mouths
Became just their sound
Filling up silent spaces between them

Maybe she felt the heat
Of all suns and all stars
Grow in the spaces between them
Universe and her body
Becoming as one
Without any spaces between them

The fingers of Fate and Destiny's drive
Pushing at her spaces between them
Whispers from Olympus
Urging her to
Reach into the spaces between them

Words from Olympus
Urging him to
Reach into the spaces between them

Voices from Olympus
Urging them to
Caress all the spaces between them

Gasps from Olympus
Surging into
The sweetest of
Spaces between them…

Will Ford

Paddy Faulkner

Paddy is an exhibited photographer, artist and film-maker, actor and performer who thinks any kind of art is a good thing because it gives people an opportunity to create, meet, & express opinions and talk about stuff other than the weather.

panopticphotography.co.uk
panopticphotography.blogspot.com
facebook.com/panopticphotography

photo: Paddy Faulkner

Stevie Stabbers

Stevie Stabbers is a very intellectual painter working in a multitude of representative and abstract styles. He is still searching to find his true voice. His early works were semiotic abstracts with influences as diverse as Manet and Frida Kahlo but now new insights have been synthesised from both those opaque and transparent dialogues.

Lowri-Claude

by
Stevie Stabbers

Don't Tell Me What to Do
by Alfero

Paddy Faulkner

panopticphotography.co.uk

photo: Paddy Faulkner

Remember: Roath is for life, not just for festivals.

– Jon Doyle, Made in Roath Blogger

Rebecca Roy

Rebecca Roy has completed the MA program at Cardiff University. She is interested in poetry and creative non-fiction, and has had several articles published in Venue magazine. To learn more about her please visit her website:

http://roypoi.wordpress.com/

or follow her on Twitter @roypoinill

Morning along Richmond Road

the harsh yelps of gulls
commence the day's feast: their cries
competing like ocean spray, break
across the pebbled backs of dormant
cars;

calling
one another in the dark, as they do
each deep blue morning
the gulls decree these streets
their hearth.

Stayed, not far from sleep
you listen
to the shore crabs emerge
to the stirring movement
of the beach.

Rebecca Roy

Susanne Koenig

Amateur Photographer based in Roath

A little rest on the way to Roath Park at one of the local beauty spots

First Prize Winner
Express Imaging Made in Roath photo competition

All the children were deliciously scared when 'Bread&Noses' appeared out of nowhere and began their mischievous act. Their performance made an already wonderful afternoon magical for adults and children alike.

Photos: Susanne Koenig

Christina Thatcher

Christina Thatcher is a PhD student and postgraduate tutor at Cardiff University where she studies how creative writing can impact the lives of people bereaved by addiction. Christina keeps busy off campus too by delivering creative writing workshops across South Wales, running projects for organizations like Making Minds and the Welsh Writers Trust, coordinating literature events for the Made in Roath Festival, and more. Her poetry and short stories have featured in a number of publications including *The London Magazine*, *Planet Magazine*, and the *Lampeter Review*. To learn more about Christina's work please visit her blog:

https://collectingwords.wordpress.com

or follow her on Twitter @writetoempower.

City Road

It shutters awake
and sleeps only
when it has to -
ripe with the smell
of shisha, mixed meats
and strong perfumes -
the road pulls us in
with its alleys
and Arabic, a deep
grace and grit bred
only in Cardiff,
embedded in Roath.
It sounds of taxis,
buses stopping,
children running,
people making art.
Its pavement keeps time
with the beat of the city,
so wherever we are
we can always hear it
calling us home.

Christina Thatcher

Photo: Rosey Brown

Mark Blayney

Mark Blayney won the Somerset Maugham Prize for Two Kinds of Silence. Poetry and stories in Agenda, Poetry Wales, The London Magazine and The Interpreter's House. He performs and MCs regularly and his one-man show 'Be your own life-coach... with ABBA' is touring. More at
www.markblayney.weebly.com

Albany Road

For a bet,
we went to the shops
wearing our long coats
and nothing underneath.

Who won the money?
Tesco.

Mark Blayney

Lake Road West

I I
was was
alarmed alarmed
to to
find find
that that
not not
only only
is is
a a
black black
swan swan
an an
unexpected unexpected
event event

but but
that that
in in
roath roath
park park
we we
have have
two two
of of
them them

who who
saw saw
that that
coming coming

```
question question
mark mark
to to
get get
over over
this this
surprise surprise
we we
eat eat
couscous
```

Mark Blayney
Previously published in The Delinquent

KARL.PRICE.MIR

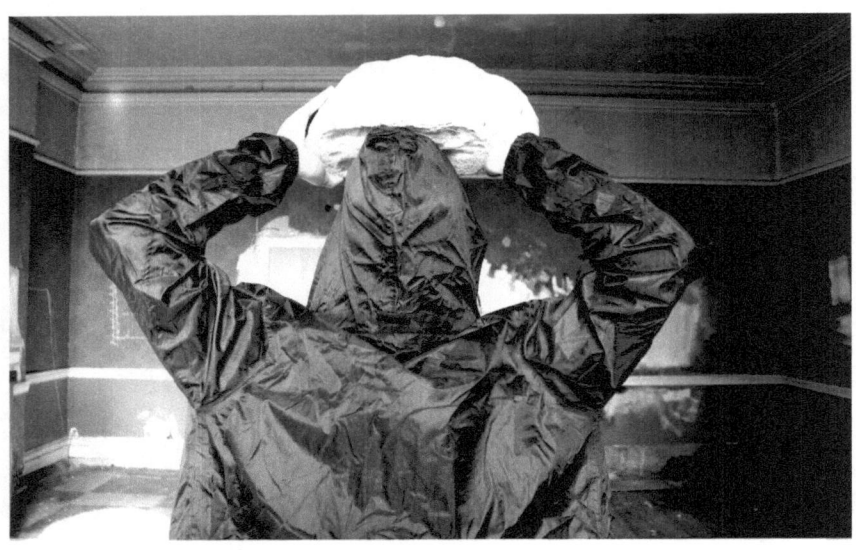

"Karl Price – MiR 2014 artist in residence.

Performed "Walk of the Lost Sheep of Roath" around streets of Roath. October 17th and 18th for 5 hours each day

Performed "between our sleep and our dreams we will make more than beautiful fossils" above Roath Park Pub on Sun 19th Oct. 12noon-5pm"

Settlement, the day long, artist-led workshop-cum-conference, cum-all-you-can-eat-buffet, was being held at the Spit and Sawdust skate park. An establishment I was not familiar with, but very impressed by. Idiosyncratic in the very best sense of the word, Spit and Sawdust has plastic dinosaurs guarding its dining tables, its burger menu scrawled on a free-standing door propped next to the counter, and a beautiful tree sculpture suspended in the middle of the skate park, for no other reason I can tell than that it looks fucking awesome.

– Rebecca Roy, Made in Roath Blogger

Sophchei
(Sophie Hickson)

SophChei is a spoken word poet who flew onto the scene in 2012. She's been described as a:

> *"Powerful, soft spoken word weaver. She appeals to 'people who like poetry' and enchants those who don't, bringing them in with her captivating, rhythmic delivery meshed with clever wordplay and alliteration".*

SophChei has been performing on open stages and slams across the UK, she won the audience prize for best performance at Cardiff Word4Word and has come in second at the Camden Hammer and Tongue slam.

She has already featured at a wealth of events including: The Moon, Raise the Bar, Papercuts the Poet, Bar Titania, Music Junkie and Troy Bar, followed by radio features on Papercuts, The Broken Verb and SpokenwordUK.

Her live performances have also seen her perform Sets at Welsh fringe festivals and Glastonbury Festival including: The Speakers Forum, Actionwork and The Bread and Roses stages.

Alongside performing, SophChei is a trained facilitator and events-organiser, with experience working with many organisations to deliver creative workshops and courses including: Actionwork, LIFEbeat, Apples and Snakes, o2thinkbig, The Free Yard and ONiiiT.

Contact details:
Email: sophiecheihickson@gmail.com
Twitter: @SophChei
Instagram: @SophChei
Soundcloud: www.soundcloud.com/SophieChei
Blog: www.SophChei.wordpress.com

Home / Gatref

A whole lifetime **o rhedeg.**

Caerdydd

Rhywle far **i ffwrdd,**
O ble fi'n meddwl I'd end up:
Familiar **a cyfforddys,**
Rhy hawdd to breathe freely, deeply.
But **fi'n nol tro ar ol tro,**
Ac tro ma fi'n weld, I see

Changes

Creativity **yn cymysgu efo** understanding,
I feel it, **fi'n teimlo fe,**
O fy mhen lawr fy nghyrff,
It's everywhere,
A bilingual assault **ar fy** memory senses:

Gatref.

Pam di bread **a menyn yn** taste **o** home?
Freshly baked melting pot
O river **melyn** soaked **i'r** crust,
Boeth i'r   **Galon**
Doughy aroma settling stomachs **a trwyn** familiar.

Traed tip toe **i** safe haven **o bara ac**   **Gymraeg**
Mixed up **yn y periant** bread,
Yn troi rownd, rownd,
Galw tongues **canu geiriau melys,**
O'r childhood **fe wnaethom i bron yn anghofio.**

Pryd oeddon newid o'r mind frame
                                             Plentyn
I
                                        Adult?
Oedolion yn cerdded a'i kneading footsteps
A shop bought **bara,**
Dim thoughts **i'r** floured footprints treading softly.

I left **amser hir yn ol i weld yr** whole **byd a'i** mysteries,
Am flynyddoedd I rejected **fy nghatref.**
Ond fy nghatref welcomed **fi nol pob tro,**
A'r comforting smells felt in nostrils **o fara ffres,**
A menyn yn melting **yn fy** mouth,
Reminds me **fi efo lle I mynd.**   I have a place to go
Home.

SophChei

Laura Amy Liderth

Laura took photos on behalf of Made in Roath and is available for freelance work.

Email: lauraamyliderth[at]gmail.com
Tweet: @lauraamyliderth

Photos: Laura Amy Liderth

Photo: Laura Amy Liderth

Do you think the setting of open house exhibitions adds something to what is being exhibited? If so, why?

Of course! It adds domestic space to the festival, which is largely about the people of Roath at the end of the day. For Made in Roath, and the art within the festival, to reach into every part and person of the community opening the private to the public is essential. The open houses bring people together, it's not just about what is shown, it's about who you meet. In entering your neighbours' houses, and allowing them to enter yours strong bonds and trust are built (in a way no other venue can facilitate) which last beyond the exhibition and festival.

Nia Metcalf
Made in Roath Open House Coordinator

Rhys John

Rhys John is a Cardiff boy with a love of writing, reading, rugby and music. A proud father of two beautiful daughters and counsellor who loves writing and reading poetry and is starting to dabble with short stories.

Passers By

The city's power of creating crowds of anonymity, people traversing other people as if they are sidestepping obstructions such as lampposts or parked cars. I sit still in a converted caravan having been given a title of 'writer in residence' and therefore feel the licence to make regular eye contact with passers- by that I would ordinarily shy away from. It's this sense of needing a reason for connection or even to give a nod or a mumbled hello, to even say something to someone that I find interesting. Situated just off the energetic snake of Albany Rd which fits snugly with my character, always just off the well-trodden paths trying to make eye contact.

It's the last session of the Made in Roath festival, the street is quiet with only the odd group or person striding past with covert eyes darting nervously in my direction. A battle of carrying on a city's status quo and the urge given by curiosity to see what's going on without being drawn in. I feel myself being weighed up, a fat man in a caravan smiling broadly at them adding to their anxiety.

To start with my children draw pictures by the typewriter as I try and add flesh to the vague bone like idea that I arrived with. To produce a poem based on the stories of the people I meet. My three year old starts her writing career by achieving an 'I' and an 'A' on the paper I gave her next to a scrawled drawing of a castle, a powerful piece.

My children leave and I am left looking ridiculously hopeful at each face that looks in, willing them to talk with me. Then three women arrive, full of cheer and what smells like recently consumed wine, I explain the reason of my being there with my own excitement at receiving my first 'customers'. They fire a limerick at me about illness and Brazilians before reflecting that Roath has many Brazilians but they don't go into that sort of pruning. The unexpectedness of the joke caught me completely off guard and I was beetroot red trying to gasp for breathe through a barrage of laughter. The women left chuckling as they went down Plasnewydd Road, I felt better now about what was to come. The ice broken by a naughty ambush joke.

I saw the well-dressed gentlemen before he saw me. His nose was buried in a festival programme and I later found out was working through as much as he could of the festival before end of day. He looked into the caravan nodded to me and came in sitting down and offering his hand to me. He made himself right at home. I stated briefly my aim and he launched straight into the story of his time in Roath. A resident of thirty two years from Surrey. He regaled me with tales of his time here, going through each address and reasons for moves. He had a magnificent poetic turn of phrase, the first flat he had returned home to find it on fire and once the fire brigade had left had entered his 'carbonised entrance hall'. His basement flat looked like a lake with the water 'gently lapping against my stereo system, adding a certain calm to the room'. He admitted to having long term mental health issues and how this affected him. He then got up and stated he better get to the next number in the book, shook my hand and was gone.

There then was a tic toc regularity of people coming into the caravan, the drunk gentleman who told me to fuck off with my Cardiff accent that made me uncertain he knew where he was. The hedonistic twenty something whose car had skidded into the street, windows billowing with that unmistakable smell and smoke of the relaxed who asked what stories I wanted because he has a million. He told me about when fifteen stealing his best friend's mother's car keys before wrapping said car around a tree. He assured me he was unscathed apart from.......this finger' He held up his hand and sure enough the middle finger was at a jaunty angle. He giggled and was gone.

I have still written a poem about this time at the shed but felt compelled to write this little piece. If any sort of art reflects life then what I took from my time at the caravan is that a person must immerse themselves in life and not simply observe from the outside. Only experience and meeting people where they are in their own environment can you learn empathy and get to see life through different eyes. I feel enriched through this experience and know that everybody has a story worthy of a mention and at the very least, a poem.

Rhys John

Footfall

Passing by in practiced anonymity,
Seeing obstructions in the faces of others.
Closed poker veneer, covert eyes taking in,
Old working class streets,
Slightly frayed but loud in experience and memories
Global stories, tinged with familiarity and creativity,
Executive rough with a soft edge,
I stopped the monotony with a smile,
Allowing people to be,
And then I entered other worlds.

Rhys John

Un-named Haiku

The City Splutters and screams
Flowing from all directions
A wall of lived silence

Rhys John

Photo: Laura Amy Liderth

Deborah de Lloyd

I love the Made in Roath festival. Every year there are interesting and exciting events and exhibitions taking place. It is a fantastic opportunity for creative people, like myself, to show off their work and get involved with the community.

In 2011 I showed my DeLloyd Designs collection at a fashion show in the Gate.

With last year's festival being bigger and better than ever, I was inspired to hold 3 events - two workshops and an open house.

One workshop was a clothes upcycling workshop with Zap Upcycled, which was held in the TAVS centre on Tavistock Street.

Zap Upcycled is a new, joint venture between two long-standing artistic friends, Melanie Hobday and myself. We are both highly experienced crafters, costumiers and designers. We share our extensive knowledge and experience through teaching and developing sewing skills and other creative techniques to others. Workshop attendees learn how to decorate, alter and re-purpose existing clothing as well as make new and exciting accessories.

I held a soft toy-making workshop as part of my main business – Cwtch Club, in Penylan library. This was a huge success with a total of 12 children attending, having fun and carrying away their own soft toy creations.

Cwtch Club's main business takes artwork made by children or adults and makes them into a 3D stuffed fabric keepsake, each piece handmade to order. I also hold toy-making workshops and parties for adults and children.

In the open house I exhibited several landscape photographs from my trip to South America, earlier that year. I also showed drawings, photographs and some of the resulting keepsakes from Cwtch Club's ever growing gallery.

It's great having this festival every year, on my doorstep, turning Roath into a hive of buzzing creativity.

cwtchclub.co.uk
facebook.com/cwtchclub
e-mail: cwtchclub@gmail.com
zapupcycled.com
facebook.com/zapupcycled
e-mail: zap@zapupcycled.com

Photos: Melanie Hobday, Rose-Marie de Lloyd

Photos: Deborah de Lloyd, Melanie Hobday

Photos: Deborah de Lloyd

Janna Grace

Janna Grace is a writer and teacher living in Alphabet City, NYC. She graduated with her MA in Creative Writing and Teaching from Cardiff University in 2013. Since then, she has run Creative Writing Workshops in Wales and around the U.S., as well as English as a Second Language at Virginia Commonwealth University. She is now freelance writing as she works on her novel and publishing her other creative fiction. Her short stories and poetry can be found in Plastik Magazine, The Bitchin' Kitsch, cutalongstory.com, and Quail Bell Magazine, among others. She is also the editor-in-chief of the online literary and arts magazine Lamplit Underground.

90 Strathnairn Street

I have a room now,
with two white curtained windows,
lined by four green wilting plants,
and three cheap framed country-scapes
above one deep backed, leaning chair
that loves to be sat in.

We all overlook the back of a school
where children scream and screech,
but only part of the day.
The rest is mine, and the mornings—
are for the seagulls.

Janna Grace

The moral of the story is to wander instead of being lost but, if you are truly lost, there are worse places than Roath during the MiR festival. Place your trust in serendipity.

– Jon Doyle, Made in Roath Blogger

Daniel-Wyn Jones

Daniel-Wyn Jones is a bilingual Cardiff-based composer whose interests include the natural drama that occurs in music and its performance. The piece acts as a dialogue between music and film in very much the same way figure in the film has a dialogue with his surroundings.

@DWJmusic
daniel-wyn.co.uk

Notes on the score:

This was produced for the collaboration I was involved with in Heloise Godfrey's Joy Orchestra Event as part of Made In Roath. There is also a still from the film I composed the dialogue for. This is essentially a joint piece from Heloise and myself.

For The Joy Orchestra
Dialogue

Daniel-Wyn Jones

Heloise Godfrey-Talbot

The Joy Orchestra

www.HeloiseGodfrey-Talbot.com

Photo: Heloise Godfrey-Talbot

Karl Price

Karl Price is an artist that mostly makes durational performance. He also makes posters, drawings, postcards, photography and ink stamps amongst other things. Price is interested in walks and collecting things he finds on the way. These objects and stories tend to be used in the making of performance and other pieces of work. The artist works in public and in more private spaces by creating environ-ments that confront fear and hope. An opportunity to create a consciousness that allows a turning to social change through warmth. Price lived in Roath several times over a 9 year period. Here he revisited the area to explore changing memories, buildings, bound-aries, and people. He gave back all that he took.

WHICH WAY ROATH

Between our sleep and our dreams we will make more than beautiful fossils

Sheltered
Shelter
Through a door
In a thin place.

A terracotta mattress
Mimics
Your rise
And demise

A woodcut
Ridicules
An etching
Thoroughly eaten out

Through spaceless crack
Acid and Metal light
To allow sculpture
Be seen

Seen
And re-seen
On a video
That never existed

Karl Price

Nigel Pugh

Nigel Pugh: Environmental social, documentary photography

Email:
nige@nigelpugh.co.uk

Website:
nigelpugh.photodeck.com

Facebook:
facebook.com/nigelpugh.photography

Twitter:
@nspugh

Photo: Nigel Pugh

Jodie Ashdown

Jodie Ashdown is coming toward the end of an MA in Creative Writing at Cardiff University. She writes poetry and prose and has also written for radio and the stage. She is a creative writing practitioner for Age Cymru and interns for Seren Books. You might see her at local open mic nights, looking nervous.

In addition to her own writing, Jodie also runs workshops. The following pieces reflect work produced in the Cardiff Alms: Re-inventing the Blue Plaque workshop which was based on writing eulogies for mostly-Cardiff landmarks.

Arnolds – Previously of Albany Road

by Jodie Ashdown

I'm sure we all remember Arnolds, a man whose magnificent dessert-making skills were so effective that I cannot remember even one thing that I ever ate for a main course. His puddings; they were fantastic.

I can picture them all now, including my favourite, the Bellybuster. An enormous mound featuring a spectacular array of flavours of ice cream, piled so high I couldn't even see over it. Monstrous in its proportions, its peaks studded with cherries, pineapple chunks, whipped cream. Then the whole thing was lovingly crowned with gallon upon gallon of chocolate and strawberry sauce.

We only ever saw him on special occasions: a birthday perhaps, or the passing of an exam. It would always take ages to find a parking spot, almost definitely to the tunes of Madonna's 'Immaculate Collection'. That's all we ever seemed to listen to.

We'd all pack into a booth; me, my brothers and all of their friends, sharing a Bellybuster with a quiver of long handled spoons. We'd dig into the centre, smear it all over our faces, shove it up our noses and around our ears. Diabetes didn't exist then, neither did lactose intolerance, or food-spread communicable diseases.

I would be in my best Minnie Mouse t-shirt, my long hair (which my brothers used to refer to as 'rats' tails') pushed back by a puffy hairband which had my name drawn onto it. I felt the bee's knees.

My mother recently informed me that the Bellybuster plates were just slightly bigger than normal serving plates, a platter at the most. And the ice cream was almost definitely budget, cheap perhaps. But to me, they were monumental, heroic in their size. They filled my dreams with their sugary expanses.

I still have the badge which Arnold gave me, saying that he loved me and that I was special. I remember him fondly. Goodbye, old friend.

Photos: Nigel Pugh

Julie Primon

Julie Primon is a current MA student in Creative Writing at Cardiff University. Originally from France, she has lived in Canada, Scotland, and India. Though her interest lies primarily in fiction (YA novels) she has lately been experimenting with nonfiction as well.

The Montbauron Open Air Pool

by Julie Primon

It is with a heavy heart that I stand in front of you today, to bid a last farewell to the Montbauron open air swimming pool.

Many of you, I'm sure, will remember the happy summer days spent playing in the water or lounging on multicoloured towels spread over the cement steps that surrounded the outdoor pool. My memories of it are like a kaleidoscope, fragmented pieces that together make a gleeful whole. I remember: the blue sky above, the sloshing of water, the shrieks of children filling the air. I remember that no matter how hot it was outside, the pool - which wasn't heated - would always be freezing. I remember the hot flush of indignation at friends splashing me, the sweet taste of revenge when they went under.

We stayed in the shallow end; the tile was always hard and cold under our feet. Sometimes we would sit at the bottom with our eyes shut tight, the air escaping our lungs one bubble at a time. The silence was eerie, all the sounds muted by water. I remember my fingers stroking over the tile, cool and close, as the seconds went by: ten...eleven...twelve...

I don't remember what my record time for staying underwater was; I'm not even sure we cared. Competition was an excuse to sink down into the smooth embrace of the pool, the quiet underwater world.

And when our teeth would start chattering, when no amount of chasing and playing would get us warm again, we would run out of the water and toward our waiting parents. The cement drank in every last drop of the summer heat and stored it jealously; it burned our feet and made swifter than we would ever have expected.

Those were good times, spent with friends around the pool. Often we would bring snacks and drinks, even picnic on the cement steps. Long, lazy days of summer fun.

When the pool re-opened after years of construction work, it wasn't the same. Oh, it was beautiful, all glass and light and carefully arranged trees around the indoor area. But the open air pool had gone. I'm sure it was deemed unnecessary - after all, the Parisian weather would not allow it being open more than two months a year - but I couldn't suppress a pang of disappointment when I realized the outdoor area was now only a long stretch of grass.

It's been ten years now. Many of the children who visit the pool have probably no idea what it once looked like. And even if they did, it's likely that they might prefer the new, sleek, modern version. But I will always treasure the memory of the time spent chatting on the cement steps, or half-laughing, half-screaming in protest when a friend grabbed my legs in the water.

The Montbauron open air pool was at once a mother and a witness to our exuberant, carefree childhood, and we will not forget her.

Julie Primon

Photos: Nigel Pugh

Photo: Nigel Pugh

The music really captures the intensity of the connection between person and object - a difficult feat for the composers to accomplish... Everyone gets talking after the show - the evening leaves us with a lot to think about.

– Rosey Brown, Made in Roath Blogger

Adam Rees

Adam is a magazine editor and freelance writer, specialising in history and angry, shouty music. Despite attempts to grow up and move away he's kept coming back to the 'Diff and now lives in Cardiff Bay.

@AdamReesy

The Llanishen Leisure Centre Slide

by Adam Rees

We are all gathered here to remember our friend, the Llanishen Leisure Centre Slide. It seems like only yesterday we were here paying our respects to the Llanishen Crocodile, that friendly yet terrifying guardian of the pool.

What's so pleasing to see is how many of you took Lil Bendy for what he was. He wasn't the biggest water slide in Cardiff, nor the fastest, and anyone with a real passion for sliding headed up the road to Pontypool or Swansea. But Lil Bendy was ours; an adrenaline-fuelled experience that had to be repeated immediately when we were youngsters, a slightly disappointing crawl to the bottom when we were older yet still so endearing. It even presented the perfect opportunity to stop halfway down and jump onto the big balls or onto your friends as they frantically tried to keep their balance atop floats during the wave machine, which we sadly now realise wasn't powered by sharks.

Whether we were having swimming lessons, wasting away summer days as part of Splash club, or going there in our teenage years because it was only 50p and you got to see girls in their bikinis, Llanishen Pool was a pivotal constant in our formative years, with Lil Bendy keeping watch over it all.

I myself fondly remember avoiding the attention of lifeguards as six of us went down him at once, dismounting in a tangled mess of limbs and laughter. I even had my first kiss under his orange gaze when I was 16, wearing bathers that left little to the imagination, and afterwards treating the lucky girl to the finest chips Cardiff Council Leisure Services had to offer.

Now the children on a Saturday morning swim with their families only have the mediocre water cannons to entertain themselves, unaware of the euphoric enjoyment of the Llanishen Slide and the wonderful, innocent memories it gave us before age, cynicism and body issues took precedent. He'll always have a place in our hearts. Don't be ashamed of shedding tears that aren't caused by my too much chlorine in your eyes.

Owain Hopkins

Owain Hopkins is a filmmaker based in the welsh valleys, working under the name Tree Top Films. He is currently in the midst of writing his first feature film which he hopes to complete before it drives him insane.

Website: treetopfilms.co.uk

Mr and Mrs Smith's

by Owain Hopkins

I wasn't sure where I was when I first heard that Mr. Smith was no longer with us. My first reaction was 'Are you sure?' and 'That can't be right?' plus many more declarations of disbelief. For someone so full of life and laughter to be taken away so soon seemed painfully unfair. Guilt soon washed over me that I hadn't visited him more often. I'm arrogant enough to hope that if I could go back and spend some more time with him, it might have kept him with us that little bit longer. But pining over a non-existent time machine now isn't going to fix anything.

We all knew he had a lot more to offer than just a friendly face. But his louder and brasher neighbours tempted us away and all the while Mr. Smith would never bend in dignity. 'This is me' he declared from his corner 'Let's have a drink'. If you ever did decide to visit him, a wall of inverted video tapes greeted you; a nameless memorial to a bygone age. I remember many a night restraining myself from bringing that monochrome monument to the ground simply to catch a glimpse of what he had there. Did he prefer Charlie or Buster? Rocky or Rambo? Or was it all just white noise? Who knows? Who cares?

But he is gone now and no amount of strong whisky is going to bring him round. He was a weekend friend; a light in the dark. And however short the time we had, I'm glad there was any time at all.

Bill Tresize

Bill Trezise is a 59 years old and is half Cornish and half Welsh. Born in Wales, he presently works as a self employed General Builder/Plumber. Writing the odd diving trip report for the BSAC Club Newsletter is 'about the extent and breadth of my writing skills, I'm afraid' he says, 'but I would like to learn.'

Llandaff Fields Public Conveniences

by Bill Tresize

Nobody mourned my closure, and subsequent demolition. I was never considered very pretty or attractive, just necessary.

I was built after the last war, in the very heart of the vast expanse of playing fields, the open air swimming pool and parklands and surrounded by major roads, schools and colleges, in a plain but very practical fashion. I was painted Council Bilious Green every year, not necessary maintenance but to cover the exaggerated graffiti, which is how young boys learned a jaundiced view of sexual reproduction from very poor illustrations.

The local Council at least acknowledged that everyone needed to spend a penny, and provided me 'free of charge' to the community.

During the day, many hundreds of children used me to change into their sports gear, out of the rain. The boys tending to use the girls side, as 'the floors were always dry'. There were no disabled toilets or babies changing facilities, as these were discouraged from the parks, as 'they were too much trouble'.

In warm weather, teenagers sat on the concrete apron under the overhanging eaves, smoking No 6 and drinking real Coca Cola (that still contained Coca extract). Local tramps, swigged scrumpy from proper earthenware flagons, and although they were smelly, unkempt and looked ferocious, they never harmed anybody.

The hours after school were normally reserved for the sexual dalliances of trainee clergy from the nearby Theological College, who were supposed to be 'batting for the other side'. I never really understood this phrase, but even the Bishop of Llandaff was arrested in a cubicle with several 'non-believers'.This caused an awful fuss and bother, and of course there was going to be a reaction.

The Council were fed up with the nocturnal exploits of the Clergy and the involvement of the Constabulary, and the ensuing publicity. They were angry at the costs of, having to constantly paint over the graffiti. Browned off with cleaning the loo's daily, and were now presented with a wonderful excuse to close them. Even the Bishop 'disrespected the facility'.

It was a sad day for any visitor to the park, who now had to run huge distances to seek relief, but there was no voice of protest to reopen the facility. I remained closed for some considerable time. Some might cynically say, until the value of the land I was sitting on was actually realised, and I was quickly sold for luxury houses.

I may be fondly remembered by many, some for all the wrong reasons.

Thanks a lot, Bish!

First I wandered along Pen y Lan road and to Alison Graham's lovely studio above The Courtyard flower shop. I arrived to hear Alison talking passionately about her ceramics. The kettle was boiling, one of her porcelain light shades cast a lovely orange glow into the room, six new shades were in the kiln and I would have been happy to curl up there all day. She tells me how the porcelain shrinks in the kiln and shows me how each is made.

- Uschi Turoczy, Made in Roath Blogger

Helia Phoenix

Helia Phoenix is a writer who mostly hangs upside down from a trapeze or hangs out at:

www.wearecardiff.co.uk.

Emporium

by Helia Phoenix

Dearly beloved,
We gather here today to say goodbye to our longstanding clubland sister, The Emporium.

A cornerstone of Cardiff's club scene during the era of the super club, the Emporium was always a guaranteed good night out if you wanted to get 'off your box' and dance until sunrise.

Yes she was smaller than many of the other clubs in town. The entry charge was often high, and bouncers unnecessarily sadistic, making clubbers stand out in the street awaiting entry while it was raining. Her walls were wet with sweat, her floor covered in a miasma of spilt drinks, cigarette butts, empty baggies and expelled body fluids, all of which were absorbed up into the oversized trousers we all wore at the time.

But we'll miss the friendly punters, and the great nights that we had there. The golden age of British breakbeat, some brilliant drum and bass, and all those nights of happy clappy house music. Her doors are closed and her shutters down, but we can all hope and pray that somewhere, in the darkness, hundreds of ravers still dance away in her, all night long.

Rest in beats.

Please be upstanding as we sing the hymn, Superstylin, by Groove Armada.

Mark Lowes

Mark Lowes is a Primary School Teacher from South Wales. Being a child of a father in the RAF, Mark moved from country to country at a young age before settling in the Vale of Glamorgan and Cardiff. He began writing from a young age but found it difficult to express himself to those around him. Since then, he has grown in confidence, experimenting with poetry, short stories and is now close to completing his first novel. The excerpt below is from this, centred around a main character with psychopathic traits who is trying to find a meaning to life.

The Writer's Shed

Hey, so, Christina [Made in Roath's Poetry and Literature Coordinator] asked me to sum up my experience in the 'Writers Shed' for 'Made in Roath', in one word – opportunity. Given my very busy schedule recently I rarely get the chance to just sit and write anymore. The opportunity presented itself when I was offered the time slot in the Shed. I didn't take much, some stories I had written, some poems, my girlfriend's laptop (because my battery is shot) and some snacks. The stories were pinned up outside for passersby, the laptop switched on, door wide open – and I wrote. It was great because it gave me that break that I so desperately needed from life. I could, once again, become immersed in my story, and while what I produced was far from my best work, it still felt good to be in the zone again.

I use the word 'opportunity' not just for me but also for others. I had some great conversations with some interesting people. Some Australian travellers wanted to feature me on their travel blog, a photographer stopped by to say, 'Hey', but the best was a man who just simply came in and sat down without introduction and smiled expectantly.

In he came, down he sat, coat on, an excerpt of my novel in his hand and he said, 'It said to pop in for a chat' (something I had written on all my prints of work pinned up outside). We spoke of his interest in writing, something which was just a spark in the dark for him at the time. He asked how I wrote, what time I did my best work, how I had gotten into the craft. I did my utmost to answer and I think I got through. We spoke about how personal writing is and how difficult it was to give your work to someone for the first time and hear their thoughts, their critique. We spoke about being open and honest and how to start. I tried to offer advice from experience, I said, 'write what you know', to start from a point which is real for you before you move onto fantastical storylines, because that, in my honest opinion, is what it's all about.

The Writers Shed was a great opportunity for me to write and for that man to speak to something who knows.

Hopefully I helped.

The following is what I wrote during my time in the Shed. To give you some context: the narrator is a man who has psychopathic traits, he doesn't feel morally or emotionally which is difficult for him. Because of this, he is trying to find a meaning to his life. He has met two people which have affected him: George, a genuine fictional psychopath, the Jack Torrance from 'The Shining' kind of deal; and Kiki, innocent, accepting, caring, etc. George has just killed Kiki. The narrator genuinely believes that evil has now triumphed over good, and is simply following the story until the end.

Thank you for reading!
Mark Lowes

Chapter 16: 'The Plan' (Wednesday, 4/9/13)

by Mark Lowes

When I started writing this, the original goal was to change people's lives. It was for someone out there, who may be struggling with the day to day aspects of reality, with the harshness of sheer boredom, to come to terms with their lives and to know that they aren't alone. This story is extreme because it's my story, and my life, after all, that is the only source of inspiration I have. I think it's more powerful than if I wrote a fictional piece and expected people to relate. No. It is extreme but extremities are necessary to paint a picture of contrast. George Harrison was my black. Kiki Driscoll was my white. As always, black triumphs to muddy the white.

Let's think back to the first chapter; I spoke about the necessary evils in the world in order for good to flourish. Without Hell there wouldn't be Heaven, if you're of the religious type. This was George's plan.

George wanted to create a utopia through dystopia. He wanted people to be stripped back to their very basic human traits, to see that technology was poison, that the media was brainwashing, that communities would thrive under severe conditions. George Harrison wondered that if you killed one, two, three people in a community, if they would band together. He wondered whether you could create a safe place for children to get back out in the street and play, if you created a slaughterhouse. He wondered if he could play God. He actually used that phrase when explaining his idea.

"We could be gods," he said. The eagerness in his eyes, the hunger, the burning desire to have control. "Fear," he said, "Keeps the world in check. But we don't want that. We want fear to free people." He didn't want to control people in the sense of regimental behaviour, rationing, et cetera. He wanted to control chaos. He wanted us to be the figure heads in a free world. "Imagine that," he practically drooled. "A world free of laws. Free of order. Free of Government. A world where you could kill for food. Money is no longer an issue; people would not work to keep the financial world ticking over. You either thrive or you die." Fear. He picked this word a lot and used it combined with freedom. I struggled, at first to see the concept, how he, who, by the looks of it, had been quietly murdering for a while, could control chaos. His plan was to free the world of modern chains, but what then? They would fight, they would die, they would eventually turn on their master, after reaching the epiphany that they could.

He wanted me and him to be the example, to create an organisation in which people simply did as they please and could not, and would not get into trouble for it. Think of a family who would look out for one another. Someone needs something done; they get it done or call in a favour. "A mafia?" I asked.

"Something like that. We would have our own family, our own world, eventually; our ideology would spread and engulf everyone."

He's talking about a revolution, like a political movement. Something which would start off quiet and then galvanise the masses, something which would recruit, which would organise, which would execute.

I was curious to see what this life would be like. Again that word: curious.

My choice was made. Kiki was gone (not completely, throughout the entire conversation between George and I, she was leaning on the table to our side). George remained. I was about to embark on the adventure of a lifetime. I was about to not just peak beyond the curtain of my abilities as an immoral human being, but take off the curtain and burn it.

What came next was George's idea of a GCSE exam. He spoke of a dystopia; it was time we initiated it. Kiki's body still lied between us. Her body slumped over the surface of the table whilst her arse was still on the chair. The wad of towel now stained red.

George nodded to Kiki when I asked how we start.

"Where?"

George said, "The best thing is to cut her up, boil her body in acid and ship her out. But considering the police are around, and she was an alibi for you earlier today, we should probably just go bury her somewhere."

Would the world be much the better place if we were meddling in its affairs? Would it thrive off our dystopia? There was only one way to find out. To wave the colour red in front of Cardiff, sit back, and watch.

George said that he would be back soon. He stood up and left my flat, and I was left with Kiki. I looked at her; her hair gathered around her head like a golden halo. I pushed it to one side; the wad of tea towel fell on the floor, and scraped back the halo to reveal her face.

Her eyes were still open, and still a deep green. Her cheeks were beginning to redden, when the heart stops beating blood around the body, gravity takes its toll and it gathers instead of circulating. She still looked alive, just frozen in a time of great pain for her. A red trickle had made its way out of the corner of her mouth.

She didn't do anything wrong. Her biggest mistake was fucking me that night. But, there's nothing I can do about that. And if I could, would I want to? Without Kiki I wouldn't have been able to give an alibi to the police, I wouldn't have been able to see the difference between her and George, and I wouldn't have been able to experience acceptance – though was I really accepted by her? She understood that I was different, yet she reacted so badly to the death of my mother.

George came back, he laid the sleeping bag on the floor and grabbed Kiki's arms, I grabbed her feet and we lifted her.

The zip concealed her face and but she was still there. Why was it that I didn't feel anything from this? That I was able to be so callous with the other extremity? Purely that she was gone, and there was nothing I could do about it. Also because, and I still firmly believe this today, that George would have killed that girl regardless of what I did that evening. He may not have murdered her in front of me, but he would have at some point. The only possible outcomes were for Kiki to die, or for George. Attacking George in that instance didn't make sense, as much as I was curious about Kiki's affection toward me, I wasn't willing to risk my life to save her. I did exactly what I said I would: I let it play out. George triumphed, evil triumphed. And I also committed to what I promised: to investigate the lifestyle of George Harrison in a hope that I would find meaning.

When you watch movies, as I did when I was a child, you don't see the heavy lifting, the sweating, the physically draining activity of lumping a body out into the hallway and into the lift. Even with two people, the dead weight of Kiki Driscoll's body wasn't necessarily hard going, but awkward. Her arse hit the floor at times. She bunched up at one end more than the other. The material we were holding also wasn't the best, it slipped under my grip. George though, his eyes, danced with life and fire. The adrenaline was coursing through his veins, whilst mine simply pumped blood.

In the lift, the sleeping bag at our feet, myself and George stood side by side, partners now.

"Quick question," I said as he pushed the large 'G' button.

"Shoot."

"How are we going to get her to her burial site?"

"One step ahead of you, my friend. I called someone to pick us up."

'Someone'. Another one of George's lackeys? Was I really special to this man, or just another monkey running around doing his bidding?

I looked up, the flies had been cleared away, the building super must have changed the bulb in there. The only death in that lift was at our feet.

"Another quick enquiry."

"Mmhmm."

"What happens if there's a family waiting on the other side of these doors when they open?"

'Ping'.

The doors opened.

A woman stood with her arms folded under her breasts. She looked about thirty, dark hair, dark eyes.

George approached her and planted a kiss on her raucous lips. It was like watching a drunk husband come home to his pissed off wife. She didn't react, she didn't kiss him back, she just accepted it with pursed lips. Her eyes didn't close, instead, they shot to me and then to Kiki who lay slumped at my feet.

She didn't question us; instead she rolled her eyes and motioned for us to follow.

George came back to me and bent to lift Kiki with me once more. "Doesn't speak English."

"What does she speak?"

"I dunno, Bulgarian, Hungarian; one of those places."

"How did you get her to come and get us?"

"I found grunting works, just make a series of intonations and she generally responds."

I stopped lifting Kiki and looked at him, he was smiling. "Taking the piss, huh?"

"Smart boy," he said.

Kiki's body was heavier than before, she was now rigid, her limbs stiffening which, in some ways, made her easier to carry.

"Are we just supposed to carry her out the front door?"

"Yes, why?"

"Looks a bit suspicious, doesn't it? She looks a lot like a dead body in a sleeping bag."

"You worry too much."

That's not something I've ever been told before. I don't think I've worried about anything too much. I have the odd moment where I try to think about every possible outcome and take the necessary precautions to not get locked up, but worried? No, that wasn't me.

Maybe George was a completely different breed to me.

And we did as he said. We walked straight out of the front door to his foreign bitch who was waiting impatiently at a red hatchback car.

She had put one of the back seats down, and had opened the boot. We laid her body into the boot and fed her through, so half her body was in the boot, the other half was in the back where I was sitting.

"You see," George said leaning back through the passenger and driver's seat. "It's all about confidence." I knew what he meant, it was about confidence. If you act suspicious, you'll be caught, if you act natural, like it was an everyday occurrence, no one would question you.

We drove without speaking. We had nothing to talk about, I had, which was odd, full faith in George's methods. He had clearly done this several times before.

We drove down busy roads, through traffic lights, stopping next to others who had absolutely no idea that a dead body lay hidden with us. I could feel that change in pace again, the beat of the heart, the increase in breathing. Not through panic, not through worry, but purely through excitement. We weren't going to get caught, we were complete control, and that was exciting.

We drove through wooded back roads, through country lanes until we stopped.

"Ok," George said opening his door. The bitch didn't, she stayed put. But George got out and walked around to the boot where he tugged Kiki's legs. I pushed the head through for him and then got out myself.

We took Kiki to a secluded. The bitter smell of the trees consumed me, the mud under my feet. All of it was very familiar. It was Arabella Reus all over again. I was in the same predicament.

George finally dropped Kiki, and panted. "Heavy bitch," he said.

I dropped her head which hit the ground with a thud. I assumed George had a way of getting rid of the body, but he casually walked away, leaving me with the sleeping bag at my feet.

I stood alone wondering whether he was coming back, he had made no indication for me to follow, but did I really need one? Had I so quickly become his lackey too? Had I done a complete u-turn on my personality and become a slave to the supposed master? I didn't know. I was unsure. I was lost. This supposed discovery of finding myself and the excitement that came with killing and control and power was brittle. I had to be very careful about everything. I had to be very careful about George and his intentions.

But now I was stuck with a body at my feet, in a sleeping bag, in the middle of fuck knows where. I could be in serious trouble with this. It wasn't Ambrose I was worried about; he was a bully, a thug with half a brain. It was James, the clever one. He would put two and two together. I could spin it. He still had George's name to go off, and after all, why would I kill my alibi?

George's footsteps crunched through the woods again, and after a moment, he appeared with a shovel which he tossed to me. "You start."

"Uh – no, you killed her, you start."

"You let her in to your home."

"I think murder beats hospitality," and I tossed the shovel back.

He grunted and started digging.

"How many people have you killed?" I asked.

George paused for a moment, his shovel in the earth, a hole appearing at his feet. He hesitated, clearly thinking about his answer.

Mark Lowes

Photo: Susanne Koenig

Last Saturday you would have found me at the Penylan Pantry, sipping black coffee, nibbling on the most exquisite walnut brownie waiting in the warmth for Penny Simpson to start her reading...Stood amongst the other festival goers, listening to her, I had the overwhelming urge to write. The type of author who inspires you to write is worth getting out of your pyjamas for.

- Uschi Turoczy, Made in Roath Blogger

Cameron Loxdale

Cameron Loxdale is a comedy writer, though I suppose that's not really for him to say. Cameron joined Roath Writers in September 2014 for an undisclosed fee on a long-term contract. He is probably best known for writing the lyrics to Outkast's hit single "Hey Ya!" which is strange because he didn't. He can be reached at:

cameronloxdale@yahoo.co.uk

as well as by post if you know his address, or in person if you know where he is and what he looks like.

How to be a Hipster

Here's a tip, be aware, take it from us.

If it's hip to be square, be a rhombus.

Cameron Loxdale

Rosey Brown

Having recently won a 2015 Literature Wales Writer's bursary, Rosey Brown now works part-time while working on her first novel, which explores the effects of extreme climate change on future life in the UK. When not writing she works for the Arts Active Trust on a variety of education and outreach projects. Rosey has lived in Cardiff for five years now, unwilling to leave after graduating from her Creative Writing MA at Cardiff University in 2014. She loves the diversity and also the familiarity of Cardiff (her mother's hometown); after two years of sofa-surfing in Roath, she is now happily settled round the corner from The Crofts pub.

City Road

Evening on City road
and the sky persists with its slow drizzle
and the pavement slabs *tip* under our feet
soaking them in grey-ish water

All along the street the smell
coriander, cardamom,
and the sizzle of roasting meat
as we walk through the windows' yellow light

and past the silent, patient gaze
of the bowling alley.

Rosey Brown

There is something inherently pleasing looking at art in someone else's living room. I think it's something to do with community spirit, realising that people are generally nice and trusting of you, making you feel nice and trustworthy when walking through their homes without grabbing their loose change or emptying their fridge. I will however admit to nosing at their book collection.

– Jon Doyle, Made in Roath Blogger

Angela Lester

Angela Lester was born and brought up in Germany. She had some of her short stories published in literary magazines and poems broadcast on Deutsche Welle radio (Literatur in Köln). After completing an MA in philosophy she came to Cardiff in 1991. She has worked as translator, cleaner and bookseller and recently published her first novel NEVER DID RUN SMOOTH, a social comedy set in Cardiff during the hot summer of 1976. Apart from writing she likes playing the piano, singing and walking in the great Welsh countryside, ideally followed by a few pints in the pub.

No Return

by Angela Lester

On a rainy afternoon in the summer of 1992 I rang the bell of 4 Longcross Street. The red paint was flaking off the door and the net curtains of the window downstairs were blackened with dirt. Mr. Qureshi, the landlord, welcomed me in.

"A nice flat," he said with a broad smile, "big and cheap."

I followed him upstairs. There had been a fusty smell in the stairwell but the windows in the living room were wide open. It was a spacious room with a television, table and some chairs overlooking the overgrown garden. I noticed straight away that the brown carpet was filthy, covered in stains, full of fluff and trodden in food.

"Just needs a bit of hoovering," he said, still smiling, gesturing towards an old fashioned looking vacuum cleaner in the middle of the room.

I nodded. Glad that the flat was within my budget, I did not look too closely at the dirty sink in the windowless bathroom or the sticky kitchen shelves as he showed me around. I had come over from Germany on a whim and was delighted to find a place straight away. I only needed a few weeks to do the research for my dissertation. A bit of cleaning wouldn't scare me off.

The terraced house had been divided into student flats, but the landlord explained that the rooms downstairs had been empty for a while. The young man who'd lived there had suddenly left, without even settling his electricity bill.

"I hope that you're more reliable," he said, shaking his head, apparently still hurt by the betrayal of his good faith.

I moved in the following morning. It took hours to clean up the place and get rid of the sticky grey coating that had settled everywhere. By the evening I was quite pleased with the result. The sun shone through the window and the room seemed homely in the peaceful evening light. I had opened a bottle of Côte du Rhone and was just enjoying my first glass when I heard a noise. It was coming from underneath the floorboards: a scratching and rustling followed by silence... My heart was beating fast. When the scratching came again I jumped up from my chair. Were there mice – or even rats? I had paid the money in advance and could simply not afford to rent somewhere else. Drinking the second and third glass of wine that evening, I made a conscious decision not to be squeamish. After the busy social life I'd had in Cologne I had not much time left and had no other choice but to concentrate on my work. I was determined to finish my research by the time I had to leave. My best friend Brigitte had announced that she wanted to visit me towards the end of my time, which was another reason to get on with it.

Every day I walked down Newport Road into the centre of town to work in the public library. The dissertation was about the perception of Germany and the German people in Britain since 1945. The librarian, a friendly lady with permed white hair, kindly showed me how to use the microfiche and I spent the first week skimming various history books as well as every newspaper article I could find. I was not surprised that there were negative attitudes after what had happened in the war, but the mistrust I came across was far worse than I had feared. Apart from the cartoon style view of the tabloid newspapers who gave the impression that Germans were all Nazis who stole sun loungers there were also more serious voices. Margaret Thatcher announced that she did not believe in national guilt, adding 'but I do believe in a national character.' Essential to the German character were 'angst, aggressiveness, assertiveness, bullying, egotism, inferiority complex, sentimentality.' And in her memoirs she added 'the true origin of German angst is the agony of self-knowledge.'

In the evenings I tried to structure the notes I had made, sipping my wine and staring through the dirty window into the dark green wilderness of the garden outside.

My thoughts kept wandering off. I saw the faces of my parents, my father's small eyes behind his glasses and my mother's smile. In the reflection of the dark window her face looked back at me, younger, the way she used to be. They hadn't been Nazis, but how could it have happened in front of their eyes? Because they had been scared – too scared to interfere or even notice what was going on? Staring at my pale reflection in the pane I asked myself what I would have done. I wished I could talk to someone about it. The mistrust of anything German seemed to me highly unfair. There was a new generation now. Didn't we all condemn acts of racism, bullying and violence – especially because of what had happened in the past?

The solitude I had been so happy about at first began to frighten me. It was a shame that the flat was at the back of the house. No noise came from outside. I lay awake for hours every night, listening to the scratching and gnawing underneath the floorboards, thinking about the German character I had been reading about.

It was the Monday night of my second week that I first heard music coming from downstairs. After yet another evening sitting at my desk, reading and writing, I had just got up to watch the news. It sounded like an aria – a schmaltzy operetta song, a male voice singing of happiness and everlasting love. The volume was turned up and I could hear every word. I stood for several minutes, unable to move. Eventually I tiptoed to the window to see what was going on. There was a light coming out of the flat downstairs, illuminating the green shrubs. Was someone living there now? When I had come back from the library earlier on the house had been absolutely quiet, the windows of the flat as always shut, the dirty net curtains unchanged. Who was listening to that awful music? As soon as the song had finished it was almost instantly played again. And as if that hadn't been enough I suddenly heard voices underneath it, a male voice groaning and a woman sobbing loudly as if in despair.

Had they moved in in the afternoon, during these two or three hours I had been away? And what was the sobbing about? Was the woman in pain? Was the man beating her? I was unable to move, still staring out of the window long after the noise had ceased. Though I went to bed early that night I couldn't go to sleep for hours, listening in the dark.

I woke up at nine. It was a beautiful day, the sky was blue and the sun lit up the room. Having a cup of tea in the kitchen, I listened to a programme on the radio about the suffragette movement before the First World War. The normality of it was calming and the fearful thoughts of last night seemed exaggerated and unreal. There would most likely be an explanation, a reason for it all. Maybe they'd just been watching something on television. I decided to knock at their door later on to introduce myself.

It was still light when I came home from the library. It had been very warm and humid all day – and now with big clouds darkening the sky, it looked as if a thunderstorm was brewing to clear the air. I immediately saw the new nameplate on the door: Mr. and Mrs. Stone. A married couple after all! The fear I had experienced the night before seemed even more silly now and I took a deep breath and rang their bell. When no-one answered I went inside. Hesitating in front of their door, I breathed in the fusty smell of the windowless hall. It was dark; the bulb had gone the week before and hadn't been replaced. I timidly knocked at the wooden door and when there was no response, a second time more forcefully. Again to no avail: no sound was coming from inside. They were obviously out.

I went upstairs and started on my evening meal, putting a frozen pizza in the oven and washing the lettuce I had bought on my way home. As it was still very close I opened the window to get a bit of air. That's when I saw the steam: white vapour coming out of the flue downstairs – a sure sign that someone was using the boiler. They were home after all. Had they seen me through the window and deliberately ignored me? My fear came back with a vengeance. Had I been right all along? I couldn't help thinking the worst. Perhaps the man had beaten up his wife so violently that she was in a bad way? I listened carefully but couldn't hear a thing, not even muffled voices from downstairs. Quietly I shut the window, afraid they might think I was spying on them.

Very tired from the night before, I went to bed early and fell into a deep sleep straight away. I was slightly disorientated when I woke up at four o'clock. Torrential rain was beating against the window and I could hear thunder rumbling in the distance. Still dazed and just about to go back to sleep, I heard a muffled bang. This time not thunder – more the sound of something heavy being dropped or thrown about. I was wide awake. After another, similar bang it was quiet again. Even the thunderstorm had moved away and the rain had stopped. For twenty or perhaps thirty minutes I sat upright in my bed, listening into the night. I was just beginning to relax when I heard the sobbing again. This time it was more distant and quiet but I had no doubt that it was the crying I had heard the night before. Images of rape and torture went racing through my mind and I thought of my parents again. Had they witnessed Jewish people being beaten up in the street? Why had no-one interfered? By the time I saw the first grey light behind the window I was determined do something and help the woman downstairs.

I couldn't go to sleep again and got up early. It must have been about half six when I left the flat to get a pint of milk. I was still upstairs on the landing when I saw the man coming out of his flat. He didn't look up and had no idea that I was watching him. He was skinny – probably in his forties – with both his arms covered in tattoos. There was a big black dog with him, a Rottweiler by the look of it. Before I could step back the dog had picked up my scent, tugged on the lead and started barking. The man turned his head, glaring at me for a couple of seconds. Then he was out of the front door and gone.

I went straight downstairs and knocked. This time I could hear footsteps, light and quick, coming near, and then she opened the door. There was a dim light in the corridor. She was wearing a pink fluffy dressing gown. I could see that she was only young, eighteen or maybe nineteen, and that her hair was bleached. "Jonathan", she cried out anxiously, looking around as if she expected to see him in the hall.

"What do you want?" She spoke with a foreign accent, Eastern European, Polish perhaps. Her eyes were wide open, the pupils enlarged.

"I live upstairs", I quickly replied, "I only want to see how you are. I saw your husband leaving the house."

She was frowning now – maybe she didn't understand. "I have no time" she let out a nervous laugh, "must go on doing household, cleaning." And then she shut the door in my face.

I bought the milk across the road and made myself a cup of tea. My hands were shaking. I could still see the man's hard face, the fear and hatred in his eyes. For a moment I wondered if I should call the police. Then I hesitated. The woman had looked scared – but wouldn't she pretend that everything was fine? And wouldn't the man guess that it was me who had told on him? What if he set that horrible dog on me? In desperate need to talk to someone about it, I phoned up my friend

Brigitte to get her advice.

"Are you sure?" She listened patiently. "You sound terrified, my God! I'll be there next weekend. Don't do anything before I get there."

She came the following Friday. I hadn't heard or seen anything of the people downstairs the last two days, but I was still really worried and burst into tears as soon as she came in.

"You look awful", she said sitting opposite me at the kitchen table. "My God, I didn't know it was so bad."

I told her again about the sobbing downstairs. "There are cases like that", I cried, "Eastern European women who are kept like prostitutes."

Brigitte looked at me with an expression of mild impatience.

"Do you really think she wants your help?" She glanced around, noticing the mousetraps I had put up. "How can you live in this dump? That awful smell! I can't believe you put up with it."

"But don't you care? I think he's beating her."

She shook her head. "There is no evidence for that. Why doesn't she run off if she's so frightened of him? You've been alone for too long. No wonder you're imagining things. You'll have to switch out of it!"

Her presence really cheered me up. She spread her things all over the flat - make-up, clothes and books. Later she poured us some wine and turned up the jazz she found on the radio. "I hope that's ok," she shouted out loud, leaning out of the window. "Sorry about the noise!" I soon stopped tiptoeing around. She made me see everything through her eyes. Maybe she was right and they had just been having sex. Wouldn't that explain it all: the sobbing and groaning and also the schmaltzy song to cover it up? Next day we went out: the first time I had been to Cardiff Castle and we walked around the Bay, where we had ice cream and several pints.

"Let's go away," she said when we came back from an Indian restaurant on Thursday night. "There are so many beautiful places in Wales. Let's go on Saturday. St. David's is only a few hours on the train."

The Saturday was very warm but overcast. A dull blanket of

clouds was obscuring the sun and from early on it was muggy and close. We'd carried our suitcases downstairs and were just about to leave, when we saw the woman coming down the street. She was wearing a shabby green cardigan which was far too warm for the weather and looked as if it belonged to someone much taller than her. But most peculiar were her sunglasses, big fashionable ones that covered nearly all her face. She walked with a slight limp and when she had to go past us to enter the house she didn't raise her head to look at us or say hello.

"Weird", Brigitte said, "she really does look weird. Mind you, the glasses are cool; I wouldn't mind a pair like them for myself."

When we sat in the train to Haverfordwest, with the trees and fields flying past, I wondered again if the girl was alright. She hadn't been limping before. Why was she hiding behind those dark glasses? But then Brigitte showed me the book about the Pembrokeshire coast she had bought at the station and I forgot about it soon enough.

St. David's was just what I needed: the walks along the coastal path with their beautiful views from the high cliffs, the sun and fresh air. We stayed for a week and every day we ate out in restaurants and pubs. I knew that there wouldn't be enough money left to stay in Cardiff, but I didn't really mind. I had done enough research and would be able to finish the dissertation in Cologne. It was a relief that the matter was out of my hands. I could see now how highly strung and confused I had been. Brigitte had been absolutely right! No wonder I had imagined things.

We came back on a Saturday. Walking down Longcross Street I could see Mr. Qureshi the landlord, standing in the street, putting black bags into his van. The front door was wide open. When he saw me coming towards him he gave me a big smile.

Have the people moved out?" I asked.

"You could say that", he replied, "terrible terrible thing!"

"What?"

"You don't know? Weren't you here last week?" He stared at me in disbelief. The woman killed herself. Fifty sleeping pills, all prescribed by her GP. She must have saved them up. The man found her lying on the floor, already cold. He was out of his mind ranting and shouting. Someone called the ambulance. They said that she was covered in cuts and bruises."

"My God, that's awful", I held my breath.

"Yes awful, terrible that's what I said." He shook his head. "Her husband said that she hadn't been right for a while. That's why she had those pills. Apparently cut herself. They do all sorts of things to themselves, people with depression. She was in a really bad way. A real shame – she was only eighteen years old. He shook his head. The man has left – no-one knows where he is. God knows how I'll get him to pay his bills."

Angela Lester

Photo: Nigel Pugh

Made in Roath must be a lot of work to organise – what is it that inspires you to keep going?

My dad always says 'it's not work if you're enjoying it'. I've come to realise that I work well under pressure which is proving rather useful! I absolutely love bringing theatre to new audiences and places outside of the traditional theatre venues.

- Rachel Helena Walsh, Theatre and Performance Coordinator

Clare Charles

Clare Charles is an artist and photographer living between Cardiff and London. She worked with the staff and drinkers in the Roath Park pub to create a hyper-local paper from their stories, as part of 2014's madeinroath. **Roath Park** is the resulting work, all the words are theirs.

RoathPark

// It used to be heaving down there, with Danny playing the mouth organ and everyone dancing and singing and dancing on the tables // Now, we're talking 35 years ago. There were skittles teams, 6 teams at least, there would be people playing every night of the week. At the weekend there was the skittle roller, which was £1 to enter, a lot of money at the time. There was 5 rows of £1 and you had to hit the highest score. You could just set on the 3 middle rows, which was cheaper, so you win the middle jackpot. Every Saturday and Sunday there would be 60/70 names up on the board and three bookmakers. The Alley Cats was the Roath Park team, can't remember if it was the Brains league or the club league. Same league that John was in... // In the 1970s there were 64 car show rooms on City Road, it was the biggest car place of the lot. The owners, they would come in every lunch time to have a drink - how much for a pint in the 70s? // You used to come here and you'd meet people from years ago. So many different landlords, but you don't understand, this is my place not their place. I've been in every room in this place, upstairs /downstairs / ladies changing. I had an accident once - not my fault - the hospital wanted me to stay in but I said No, I'm going to where I go every day. I had to drink out of the corner of my mouth. I stayed that night in the pub, up in the hotel rooms where the officers stayed in the war. Oh yes, the Blue Room they called it, that upstairs space //

I don't know what will happen to this place. They can't turn it in to flats, there's no parking. It's no good as a food place, there are too many food outlets. No parking, no passing trade **//** Barbados is crap, don't bother **//** We used to play a game called Nap, honestly, I can't tell you how much stuff we used to do here. It was one of the most important and influential things that happened in this pub. John, the landlord at the time, would only have four people playing. Win five hands, no 2, 3, 4, 5, 6, 7, 8 - only top cards. There was a banker - 10p to look, double up at the end. Last time I won £55. Everyone couldn't wait to be able to play **//** He's a good mate, and a good mate is hard to find. I won't mention that I used to go down to the bottom **//** I'd go in the lounge and he's in there and she's in there, 'Get out of here' and I'd end up sitting there with them telling lies. They'd say 'why do you upset me, why do you have to go and upset the great queen?' I could name them all here, and when I say good... **//** Everyone paid a pound and we bought a bottle of Jamison's, the youngest (that was me) had to go out and give it to the winning side **//** Brenda came in one day, she'd said they had some Jack Russell's up in Diana Street, said she wanted a Jack Russell. She brought her in here, I said That's not a Jack Russell! The paws were bigger than my fucking head! She had it for three weeks, it doubled in size, clinging on to everyone. Used to pull her around - it would be all over you. You could see it was a greyhound, so comical she used to say 'It's my Jack Russell' **//** It's my heart, nothing can buy it. Nothing can match the people I've met here **//** Get your ass out there. That's why I love Cardiff. It's the best civic centre in Europe. Everyone wanted to come and see it. Look at the Museum, look at this. For me, Cardiff. I'll be an Irish man till the day I die, but if anyone says anything against Cardiff **//** I can remember going to my grandma's house, her door was held open with a latch, never closed. Her hearth was as black as the ace of spades, always cooking, something baking and something on the side, and I couldn't wait, I couldn't wait. I fought a couple of kids down in school this time, 'Is this your grandson there' their mum said 'look at what he's done to my sons'. And they were massive! Massive. They'd picked on me because I was wearing my satchel and hat **//** Karen Carpenter, one of my favourites **//** Jesus Christ I've got so many memories of Cardiff. Something like that nobody can buy **//** The greatest thing in love is having a enjoyment of the people you sit down with and a good beer **//** I've sat in the bus stop with them and wonder why 20/30 years ago 'you alright?' 'you alright?' Nobody knows what's happening now. Trust me, whenever I was in a bus stop it was 'you alright?'. And some days you're worried, seems they don't give a shit. Have a look, have a look at City Road **//** I have a great belief in life. I came here in 1961, I will always love Cardiff till the day I die. Don Sheppard took 2000 wickets in 1969, so I'm not telling a lie, and I know that, because I lived around the corner. You know, you can only drink so much **//** I am telling you the gospel truth, I am the bollocks. It's not because I says it, no, it's because I love this place. My memories, I tell you

something young lady, I will always miss my
mates, young lady. Whenever we met, if he
said shit then I said shit. I'm not saying
anything, I've had more fun here than I've
had in 30 years. Honest to god, I've done my
bit for now! // This is in my old pub now, I
used to have a parrot behind the bar, Murphy.
Anyway, I had this massive teddy bear, one
of these ones that you give away in a raffle,
and he was up on the bar next to Murphy. He
was there for ages, 4 months maybe more, and
eventually this guy won him. When I went to
get it for him, all the stuffing came out of
the arm next to Murphy's cage. He'd been
eating away at him, and all Murphy could say
was 'oh fuck, oh fuck'. He picked up some
terrible language. I had to sell him in the
end because of the grandchildren. A man up
in London bought him, to breed with his
birds, but they were outside and I said you
can't do that as he's used to being in. So
this man bought him, and was taking him out
two minutes the first day, five the next.
Anyway, I got a phone call from him saying
he's made a mistake, because every time
someone knocked at the door his 17 parrots
started saying 'Fuck, fuck, fuck'. Murphy
had taught them all to swear // I'm telling
you a story you've got nothing to do with.
When you live someplace, when you are born
someplace, and you leave, there's no back
door, like I ran out there taking blood.
Don't ever tell me you don't miss it. But
it's all different. Me, I can't, I don't
know where to go. It's not what I want, no
disrespect to you. I had a great thing a few
years ago, and I went home. It didn't work.
It didn't bloody work. The people, they had
the bottle to stay there. To look after it.

Nobody in the world can buy that. Because they are real people, they look after the heritage. I watched a programme, man with dog, or two dogs, living in Snowdonia. And he might come down for the game or whatever, but nobody can buy it. And it's the same in every country **//** Who's this? Ronan Keating? I think he's marvellous. He's the worst fucking singer I've ever heard **//** By the way, put this in, don't bet on me **//** Good night, may the good Lord go with you. No! You've got a lot more than you worked for. Good night. **//** He's a good man, and a funny bastard, and a good man **//**

Clare Charles with the staff and drinkers in the Roath Park pub

This is my very first Made in Roath so I had the strange advantage of going in blind, never having attended the events that the objects were attached to. What I found [at Storio – Store] was a starkly simple exhibit of carefully labelled and bubblewrapped 'memories', if you like. (The handlist was an essential part of the exhibit, might I add). And something very peculiar happened. Even though I had no prior knowledge of these souvenirs or their context, I could imagine hearing and smelling and seeing the memories housed behind the muffled plastic; song books and prompts and jugs and even a parasol from the late Kim Fielding used as part of Naked Lunch in MiR 2012. In the silence, these echoes suddenly became loud again.

- Sara Bellanato, Made in Roath Blogger

Made in Roath

Made in Roath is warm
like buttered toast and
just a short flight from
the Sugar Loaf;

Quite near to the park
It lightens the dark
with arts so fine you can
drink them like wine;

Fine wine for a window
from which to grow,
to see some light on
cold autumn nights;

Lights of humour and
bared souls, nights
of laughter and fearsome
ghost stories told;

Some music and magic
songs, rhyme and verse
sometimes with little time
to rehearse;

But perfection is not
what it's meant to be,
but making some friends
for a warm community.

Fran Smith

Photos: Nigel Pugh

Dave Daggers

After recovering from the Royal College of Art Dave Daggers dabbled for many years failing at photography, ukulele playing, body-painting and life-drawing. He then decided to dabble with words. His poetry is always shallow, meaningless and never says anything about his life, his beliefs, or his personal psyche. UNTILL TONIGHT Dave Daggers.... Will perform poems about his own successful suicide, about sexy French Girls, about haunted iphones, and even poems about poems that don't exist email is dave@davedaggers.com

Sweaty in Roath Cardiff

There's a trough of low pressure over Roath Cardiff

They're expecting scattered showers over Kathmandu

It's been snowing in Vancouver

But I'm still hot and sweaty over you

There's a fissure in the continental shelf

and a tidal wave's about to hit the coast

I'm running hard to save myself

But it's you I want to save the most

I'm drenched to the skin

As I struggle through the monsoon

I'd call you but the phones don't work

And the telephone wires are all strewn

Hummmmmmm

There's another dust storm in the Sahara

There's a coup-d'état in Salvador

I like the girl who sells tobacco on the corner

But you're the one that I adore

A meteors going to hit the Earth

And I don't know what to do

My thoughts are all about death and birth

And the times I've spent with you

The Martians have invaded town

And the death rays aiming at me

I'd get a gun and shoot them down

But its with you I'd rather be

There's a tsunami in the Pacific

And its gonna drown all of us

But I still think you are terrific

In fact you're fabulous

There's a trough of low pressure over Roath Cardiff

They're expecting scattered showers over Kathmandu

It's been snowing in Vancouver

But I'm still hot and sweaty over you

Dave Daggers

Photo: Nigel Pugh

Jill Berrett

Jill Berrett is a writer of poetry, short stories, and memoir. Through the process of her writing she seeks to disclose what is often hidden in peoples apparently ordinary, but sometimes surreal, daily lives. Her work has become a thread between her younger and older self. She has read her work at various events around Cardiff, including, recently, at the launch of the Modern Alchemists exhibition Solve et Coagula, an exciting experiment bringing artists and writers' work together. Roath has been Jill's home of choice for over 3 decades and makes regular appearances in her work.

Writer's Shed

Saturday 18th October 2-3 p.m.

This was my first experience of a writers' residency so it felt exciting and a bit nerve-wracking as to how best to use the opportunity. I have this idea about democratising poetry, taking it out to people who might think that it's something that isn't for them, for whatever reason, so I decided this would be my aim.

I printed up a range of my poems, wrote signs with themes like loss, love, disability, politics, and mothers, and with Renn's help we stuck all those on the outside of the caravan. On the table outside I put a couple of poetry books for children and adults, our anthologies, and a book of poetry that my mother won in 1922! A couple of friends came along and read both inside and outside the caravan.

The idea was to generate an exchange between people passing, encouraging them to think about stories that might be inside them, and about writing. With there being a lot of stalls at the Roadblock it was very busy with passers-by so I read my poetry walking up and down the street. Some people stopped and listened, a few even clapped which was encouraging.

Quite a few people stopped at the caravan and read my poems. I chatted with them about universal themes that we might share. With a couple of people who were interested in a particular theme I read aloud to them, which they seemed to appreciate. I also talked to children about what they liked.

Even though a lot of people were just walking past as I read aloud I felt it was still worthwhile using public space in this way. Children, in particular, were curious, and who knows what gets absorbed as people pass on by?

JILL BERRETT

Stevie Stabbers

Photo: Nigel Pugh

Mab Jones

Mab Jones is like a kind of mythical creature who has torn up all the leaflets and put them in a bucket – then she has tipped the bucket off the roof of the Albany Road Tesco onto the heads of the hordes of hipsters drifting past on their mini-segways.

Crikey – she has taken over the poetic world of Wales and turned it into Mabland – she's even been a writer-in-residence in Dylan Thomas's Boathouse for Mab's sake.

<u>Elm Street</u>
Sugar pink, baby
Blue – sweet dreams, maybe, behind
The lidded windows.

<u>City Road</u>
Silken dresses hang
On display, like promises
Waiting to be kept.

<u>Wellfield Road</u>
Well-to-do woman
Drops two pennies on the ground –
Her final purchase.

<u>Albany Road</u>
Shopping in one hand,
Child in the other – a list
Of things still to do.

Mab Jones

More info about
Made in Roath
and about
the bloggers,
co-ordinators,
organisers and
contributors
on the
website
at:

http://madeinroath.com/